MILLIONAIRES FOR JESUS
The Love of God in Poems

OLIVER F. FULTZ SR.

ISBN 978-1-0980-4753-5 (paperback)
ISBN 978-1-0980-4755-9 (hardcover)
ISBN 978-1-0980-4756-6 (digital)

Copyright © 2020 by Oliver F. Fultz Sr.

All rights reserved. No part of this publication may be reproduced, distributed, or transmitted in any form or by any means, including photocopying, recording, or other electronic or mechanical methods without the prior written permission of the publisher. For permission requests, solicit the publisher via the address below.

Christian Faith Publishing, Inc.
832 Park Avenue
Meadville, PA 16335
www.christianfaithpublishing.com

Printed in the United States of America

His Voice

Oh, Lord, I love to hear your voice as you speak to me each day words of comfort, peace, and joy before I start my day. I'm waiting for your instructions to find my way you see so I will know just what to do to set the captives free. I need your holy word, my Lord, to guide me as I go into the streets so I will say what you want me to say to everyone I meet. You are so loving and so kind. Your voice to me is sweet, clear, and true.

Our Holy Mother of Zion

She was truly our Holy Mother of Zion—her love and faith in God was as strong as a mighty lion.

For many years, she lived a holy and sanctified life. She was a holy mother and a holy wife. She taught all of her children to kneel, pray, and walk with Jesus leading the way. The steps she made in life were clean and pure. The precepts she expressed were righteous and sure, and the examples she taught us will long endure. It was the Holy Ghost that made her life complete and the love of God in her life that made her so sweet. Truely, she was our Holy Mother of Zion. Her love for God was as strong as a mighty lion. It was obedience to God's word that guided her feet and her daily prayer life that kept her sweet. She taught me how to kneel and pray and always said, "Let Jesus always lead the way for He is the way the truth and the life." Mother Selena Layne was a holy mother and a sanctified wife. She taught us all how to live the sanctified life because her life was controlled by Jesus Christ.

His Voice Part II

Have you ever heard the whispering wind or the sound of rolling waves flowing in as water rushes upon the shore or a strange knock upon your door? Then you go to the door and see no one, but the sound you heard was pure and true—the voice you heard was just for you. It wasn't old and it wasn't new. It was the voice of Jesus that spoke to you.

His Voice Part III

Sometimes you can hear it in the falling rain. If you listen intently, it's very plain. He says, "Be still and know that I am God." What does he really mean? No matter what's going on in your life, be very still and listen for His holy voice. He will speak peace into your heart, mind, spirit, and soul: "My son, my daughter, I'm still in control."

From the Holy Spirit, a Song

Be Still and Know That I Am God

Be still and know that I am God. No matter what you're going through, my love will always be with you. I walked the streets of Galilee and shed my blood to set you free. Be still and know that I am God. Be still and know that I am God.

No matter what you're going through, my love will always be with you. I walked the streets of Galilee and shed my blood to set you free. Be still and know that I am God. Be still and know that I am God. No matter what you're going through, my love will always be with you. I walked the streets of Galilee and shed my blood to set you free.

I Need You Now

I need you to know me now
I need you to show me how
I need you now
I need you to take my sin
I need you to bring me in
I need you to be my friend
I need you now
I need your holy voice
To make the righteous choice
I need you now
I need your holy mind
I am no longer blind
It is your great design
Now I am free

You shed your blood for me way back at Calvary. I have the victory. I know you now. I have your peace and joy given to me as a baby boy. I need you now.

You gave me love and joy even as a baby boy. I love you now. Many mothers held me tight and sang to me day and night. They gave me your love. I love you now. Your love is holy and true. It makes the old brand-new. Your love is you.

You are the holy Son who died for everyone. Your love is true. Your name is Jesus Christ, Creator and Lord of life. The holy seed of love who came from up above (John 6:33)—the Father's chosen one, the holy Living Word. You are the Bread of Life (John 6:35). You took my pain and strife; you gave me life.

You are the Holy Son, the everlasting Living Word. You are my Son. I sent you down to man. They just don't understand why I sent you. You came into the earth to give all men new birth to know what they are worth. You shed your blood for me way back on Calvary. You are my Lamb. You are my Holy Seed, my Lamb that had to bleed. I need you now. I need your hands and eyes to help me realize just how great you are. I need you now in my soul to help me take control. I need to know your heart to get a brand-new start. I need you now. I need you on my mind part of your great desire to show me you, your holy way of love that came from up above. I know you now. I hear your holy voice. It is my only choice. You've chosen me.

Now that I have your love; it came from up above and touched me like a dove. I love you now. I know your love is true because it came right from you. You are my Lord and King, your holy hands made everything with your precious blood—you bought my soul.

The Gospel of Love

The gospel of love is Jesus, my Son, who I sent to die for everyone. The gospel of love is my Holy Seed, my Holy Lamb that had to bleed. He shed his blood on Calvary. Believe in Him and be set free. The gospel of love is my Holy Light. He shed his blood to make things right. The gospel of love is my Holy Lamb. The gospel of love is my Holy Lamb. My gospel of love is the Great I Am. My gospel of love is the risen Lamb.

My gospel of love is my righteous Son who gave his life for everyone. My gospel of love is my holy choice. Listen to him and hear my voice. The gospel of love is my holy seed. I sowed Him in, to meet all your needs. His holy hands made everything. He caused the bells of freedom to ring. This nation is now blind and has lost its way, out of darkness into day. My gospel of love won't let you down.

To every little girl and boy—my gospel of love is holy and true. My gospel of love is calling you. He's calling you and me to stand and lift up every fallen man to bathe them in His holy love that only comes from up above. He reaches deep into the soul and causes His love to take control, bringing peace and joy into the mind, erasing doubt and bringing faith in line. Faith and hope are a part of me that will always set the captives free.

My gospel of love is holy and true. My gospel of love is calling you. He's calling you and me to stand and lift up every fallen man, every woman boy and girl that ever comes into the world. My gospel of love is my Holy Son who I sent to die for everyone. I sent Him down to set men free. Then He shed his blood on Calvary; believe in Him and come to Me.

My gospel of love always honors me. To those who receive him, there's victory. You must open your heart to my Holy Son who gave His life for everyone. It is written in John 3:16 and John 1:1, "Believe in Him and come to me through my son. My Holy Son, who will set you free!" Free from sin, death, hell, disease, and pain. He will heal your body and also your brain.

The gospel of love is Jesus, my Son, who I sent to die for everyone. The gospel of love is my Holy Seed, my Holy Lamb that to bleed. He shed his blood on Calvary. Believe in Him and be set free. The gospel of love is my Holy Light. He shed his blood to make things right. The gospel of love is my Holy Lamb. My gospel of love is the Great I Am. My gospel of love is my righteous son who gave his life for everyone. My gospel of love is my holy choice. Listen to Him and hear my voice. The gospel of love is my Holy Seed. I sowed Him in the earth to meet all of your needs. His holy hands made everything. He caused the bells of freedom to ring. This nation is blind and has lost its way, out of darkness into day. My gospel of love won't let you down. He reaches all the way to the ground. My gospel of love will calm the floods. My gospel of love made the land and sea.

My gospel of love came out of me. My gospel of love is holy and bright. My gospel of love rules the day and night. My gospel of love will make you wise. My gospel of love has healed your eyes. My gospel of love knows the great and small. My gospel of love belongs to all. My gospel of love brings peace and joy to every little girl and boy. My gospel of love is holy and true. My gospel of love is calling you. He's calling you and me to stand and lift up every fallen man and bathe them with his holy love that only comes from up above. He reaches deep into the soul and causes his love to take control, bringing peace and joy into the mind, erasing doubt, and bringing faith in line. Faith and hope are a part of me that will always set the captives free.

He frees us from death, disease, and pain. He's someone who doesn't have to be explained. My gospel of love is Jesus Christ, the source of all life and the seed of all life. He's the Alpha and Omega—the first and the last, the beginning and the end. Make Him your choice! He's better than a friend. Jesus is my gospel of love.

The Seed of Love

Jesus Christ is God's seed of love. He was sent to earth from heaven above. He walked the streets of Galilee and showed men how to be like me. I am His Father, and He's my son. He shed his blood for everyone. He is your way to eternal life. You know Him best as Jesus Christ; He is God's seed of holy love. He was sent by me to deliver true love. Won't you please believe in my only Son? He shed His blood for everyone, the blood He shed for me. I asked Him to do it to set you free. Won't you please believe in my Holy Son. He came to earth for everyone. He is my way, my truth, and my life. You know Him best as Jesus Christ.

Won't you please come to hear my son. I sent Him to speak to everyone. If you don't hear Him, you cannot hear me. If you can't see Him, you cannot hear me. If you can't see Him, you cannot see me. Believe in Him and become my Son. He shed his blood for everyone. If you accept Him, you'll receive my love and life and become one of my sons through Jesus Christ.

He's coming back to earth one day very soon, I have to say. You'd better pray and give Him your life. He took your pain, your sins, and your strife. Just believe in my Son and receive my love. I sent Him to you from heaven above. Won't you please believe in my Holy Son? I sent Him to die for everyone. He paid the price for you and me. Believe in Him and be set free, and then you'll have victory.

Jesus

Jesus, you have called me and chosen me to win. Jesus, you have saved me and cleansed me from my sin. Jesus, you have kept me from danger deep within. Jesus, you're my Lord and Savior and also my Best Friend. Lord, how I adore your holy name. You are always God alone, and always you're the same.

Lord, you are so holy, so righteous, and so true. Deep down with my soul, you've made all things brand-new. Lord, why do you love me just the way you do? The reason why you love me is just because you're you. Lord, I want to please you and praise your holy name. You're my Lord and Savior. I love to praise your holy name. Lord, you are so gracious, so holy, and so divine. Lord, you are so righteous, so holy, and so kind. Lord, you are the King of kings whose hands made everything with your great love for all mankind.

Your son has set us free because of all the blood He shed. We have victory. I thank you, Lord, for your great love and how you brought me out. It is you and in you alone, Lord, I have no doubt. Because of you and your great love, my soul can really shout. You have washed my soul deep within and also out.

The Kingdom of God

The kingdom of God holds the kingdom of love. He came down to earth from heaven above. He walked the streets of Galilee and shed His blood to set men free. When He died on the cross at Calvary, He gave all men the victory. When Jesus Christ was crucified, the debt for all sin was satisfied. He satisfied His Father, you see.

My Kingdom of Love

My kingdom of love is Jesus, my Son, who I sent to die for everyone. On the third day, He arose from the dead. And He's also known as the Living Bread. He is my holy light, you see. Believe in Him, and come to me. I am His Father, and He is my Son who I sent to speak to everyone.

If you don't listen to Him, you cannot hear me. My voice is heard when you hear my Son. I sent Him to speak to everyone. He is my only message of love that came to earth from heaven above. My son is the only way to me. I sent Him to set the captives free, and now they have the victory.

I sent him to fill the law with life to take your sins and bear your strife and also give you life. My Son is the living water and the living word of life. I sent Him to deliver my love that I sent to earth from heaven above. I am in Him, and He is in me. Read John 17 and you will see.

The True Vine

Jesus Is the Vine—Followers Are Branches

"[a]I am the true Vine, and My Father is the vinedresser. Every branch in Me that does not bear fruit, He takes away; and every *branch* that continues to bear fruit, He [repeatedly] prunes, so that it will bear more fruit [even richer and finer fruit]. You are already clean because of the word which I have given you [the teachings which I have discussed with you]. Remain in Me, and I [will remain] in you. Just as no branch can bear fruit by itself without remaining in the vine, neither can you [bear fruit, producing evidence of your faith] unless you remain in Me. [b]I am the Vine; you are the branches. The one who remains in Me and I in him bears much fruit, for [otherwise] apart from Me [that is, cut off from vital union with Me] you can do nothing. If anyone does not remain in Me, he is thrown out like a [broken off] branch, and withers *and* dies; and they gather such branches and throw them into the fire, and they are burned. If you remain in Me and My words remain in you [that is, if we are vitally united and My message lives in your heart], ask whatever you wish and it will be done for you. My Father is glorified *and* honored by this, when you bear much fruit, and prove yourselves to be My [true] disciples. I have loved you just as the Father has loved Me; remain in My love [and do not doubt My love for you].If you keep My commandments and obey My teaching, you will remain in My love, just as I have kept My Father's commandments and remain in His love. I have told you these things so that My *joy and* delight may be in you, and that your joy may be made full *and* complete *and* overflowing.

Disciples' Relation to Each Other

"This is My commandment, that you [c]love and unselfishly seek the best for one another, just as I have loved you. No one has greater love [nor stronger commitment] than to lay down his own life for his friends. You are my friends if you keep on doing what I command you. I do not call you servants any longer, for the servant does not know what his master is doing; but I have called you [My] friends, because I have revealed to you everything that I have heard from My Father. You have not chosen Me, but I have chosen you and I have appointed and I have appointed you and placed purposefully planted you, so that you would go and bear fruit *and* keep on bearing, and that your fruit will remain *and* be lasting, so that whatever you ask of the Father in My name [as My representative] He may give to you. This [is what] I command you: that you love *and* unselfishly seek the best for one another. (John 15:1–17, AMP)

A Message from the Father

My love is speaking to you today. He's speaking to you in a special way. I say to you, my righteous Son, "Please share my love with everyone. My love is pure, strong, and right. My love rules the day and also night." My love is just the thing for you. My love makes old things new. My love is holy, bright, and true. He's the one who's keeping you. He watches over you, day and night and opens your eyes with holy sight.

My Love

He will walk along with you today and tell you things that you must say to each person that comes your way. My love is like a healing balm. It takes the rage and brings the calm. My love is mighty strong and rue. My love is the one leading you. He's leading you each day and night and guiding you with His holy light. He's saying speak my word with my holy love that I have given you from up above.

My love to some is still unknown, but He will never leave you alone. He's the one who created the earth. I sent Him to you with a holy birth. He walked the streets of Galilee and showed men how to live for me. He's speaking to you right now my Son, saying, "Please share my love with everyone. My love builds, renews, and lifts. It's one of my most holy and righteous gifts.

"My love never puts anyone down. He reaches all the way to the ground. He enters the very heart of men and shows them how they can win. Win the lost with my love alone and lead them to my most holy throne." There's nothing on earth just like my Son. I sent Him to earth for everyone.

He's saying to all, "Come to me, and my love will set your spirit free." Free to accept my Holy Son that I gave for everyone. Jesus is my Holy love.

Why Jesus Came

Jesus came into the earth to change the hearts of men. To shed His blood on Calvary's cross and bring the lost souls in, into his church, which He built Himself upon His holy name. I'm speaking to you today, my Son, to get your ear again. You must go out and share my love with every fallen man. Men who do not know that Jesus is my love, that I sent Him into the earth from heaven up above.

He came down to obey my word and do my holy will. When He shed His blood on Calvary's cross, He paid the buyback bill. The price He paid was just enough for me. By shedding His blood on Calvary's cross, He set the captives free. They got up from their tombs and walked upon the earth. This showed the world what His blood could do when He split upon the earth.

If men would just believe my Son and receive my holy love, I'll give them all a brand-new birth from heaven up above. Won't you tell them all, my Son, the reason why I came? If you don't obey my word, it would really be a shame. This word is coming to you, my Son, right from my holy throne. Please go out and share my love to bring the lost souls home.

My love is still unknown to some. My son—it is He you see. He's the one who shed his blood to set the captives free. Free from death, disease, doubt, and also unknown pain. If men would accept his love, they have much to gain. This is why Jesus came. These words are not meant for you alone. They come right from my holy throne. They're meant for you to share with people you meet everywhere. As you go along your way, please share my holy word and love every day. This is all I have to say. Obey my word, my Son.

My Son is the resurrection and the life. Anyone who accepts him and believes in him will obtain everlasting life. They will never die. They will love with me eternally. They will also eat from the tree of life and live forevermore. My name is Jesus, and I am the way to the tree of life and also its source. I am coming back very soon. Be ready.

The Revelation of the Shed Blood of Jesus Christ

(Key scripture: John 3:16)

For God so love the world! What does the word *world* mean? It means all of mankind! Every kind of man on earth! Every man, boy, or girl born of a woman on earth. When Adam sinned in the garden of Eden, he separated himself and all men born after him from God. He was no longer in God's image like God with God's moral character and image. When he sinned, he disobeyed God and become like the one. He obeyed that is Satan, the devil. He also gave Satan all the things that God gave him dominion over in the world. He was now a son of the devil because his refusal to obey God. His act of disobedience totally separated him from God. He actually died—that is, he was no longer united to God spiritually—his relationship with God was broken. John 3:16 says, "For God so loved the world, all men that He gave Jesus to the world to die for all of men's sins. To become sin for all men born of a woman."

Jesus Christ is God's Holy Son with God's holy blood in his body. The holy blood of God's only begotten Son had to be shed on earth to remove all sin from all men born of a woman. For the scripture says, "Without the shedding of blood, there is no remission or removal of sin." The shedding of the precious blood of Jesus was all that God, the Holy Father needed as payment for the sin of every man born of a woman. He gave his only begotten son that whosoever believeth in him—that is, Jesus shall not perish but shall have everlasting life. Only the blood of Jesus could redeem mankind from sin or Satan, the father of sin. When Jesus was on the earth, He said these words: "I am come to do the will of Him that sent me." He also said, "I always do those things that please the Father." When we become the children, when we accept Jesus Christ as our Lord and Savior, we become the children of the true and living God. His shed blood on the cross gives us sonship to the Father through the Son. Jesus said in John 14:6, "I am the way, the truth and the life. No man comes unto the Father accept my by me." John 3:17 says, "For God sent not his Son into the world to condemn the world, but that the world through him might be saved. He that believeth is not condemned. But he that believeth not is condemned already because he hath not believed in the name of the only begotten Son of God." Matthew 1:18–21 says,

> The Birth of Jesus Christ was on this wise when his mother, Mary was espoused to Joseph, before they came together, shew as found with the child of the Holy Ghost. Then Joseph her husband, being just a man and not willing to make her a public example was mined to put her away privately but while he thought on these things, behold the angel of the Lord appeared unto him in a dream saying, Joseph thou son of David, fear not to take unto thee Mary thy wife, for that which is conceived in her is of the Holy Ghost. And she shall bring forth a son and thou shall call his name, Jesus for he shall save his people from their sin.

The Character of Love

When the son of man come in his glory, and all the holy angels with him, then shall he sit upon the throne of his glory:

> And behold him shall be gathered all nations: and he shall separate them one from another, as a shepherd divided his sheep from the goats. And he shall set the sheep on his right hand, but the goats on his left. Then shall the King say unto them on his right hand, come be blessed of my father, inherit the kingdom prepared for you from the foundation of the world. For I was an hungered and ye gave me meet: I was thirsty and you gave me drink I was a stranger, and ye took me in naked and ye clothed me; I was sick and ye visited me: I was in prison and ye came unto me Then shall the righteous answer him saying Lord, when saw we thee and hungered and fed thee? Or thirsty and gave thee drink. (Matt. 25:31–37)

> This was done that it might be fulfilled which was spoken of the Lord by the prophet saying Behold a virgin shall be with a child and shall bring forth a son and they shall his name Emanuel, which being interpreted is God with us Then Joseph being raised from sleep did as the angel had bidden him and took unto him his wife and knew her not till she had brought forth her first born son: and he called his name Jesus. (Matt. 1:22–25)

The Qualities of Love

Though I speak with the tongues of men and of angels and have not love, I become as a sounding brass or a tinkling cymbal. And though I have the gift of prophecy and understand all mysteries and knowledge and through I have all faith so that I could remove mountains and have not love, I am nothing. And though I bestow all of my goods to feed the poor and though I give my body to be burned and have not love, it profit me nothing. Love suffereth long, and is kind, love envieth not; love vaunted not itself, is not puffed up doth not behave itself unseemly seeketh not her own, is not easily provoked, thinketh no evil. Rejoice not in iniquity but rejoyceth in the truth bareth all things believeth all things, hopeth all things endureth all things love never faileth but where there be prophecies they shall fail, whether there be knowledge, it shall vanish away For now we know in part and we prophesy in part but when that which is perfect is come, then that which is in part shall be down away when I was a child, I spake as a child, I understood as a child, I thought as a child but when I became a man, I put away childish things For now we see through a glass darkly but then face to face: Now I know in part but then shall I know even as also I am known and now abideth faith, hope, love, these three but the greatest of these is love. (1 Cor. 13:1–13)

Who Is Love?

Jesus is love: He is the source of all life. He is the Creator of all things. And by Him and through Him, all things are held together. He is the most powerful force in the world. By the word of the Lord were the heavens made and all of the host of them by the breath of his mouth. Now let us deal with the word *gospel*. The word *gospel* means "good news." Most news that we hear today is not good because it is of the world. But in John 3:16 of the Word of God, it is recorded the good news for all mankind, for every man on earth (John 3:16)—the *world*, meaning all mankind that He gave every man on earth His only begotten Son that whosoever believeth in Him should have everlasting life. This is the good news of the meaning of the "gospel of love." The "gospel of love is Jesus, my Son" who I sent to die for everyone. The gospel of love is my Holy Seed, my Holy Lamb who had to bleed. He shed His blood on Calvary. Believe in Him and be set free. The gospel of love is my Holy Light. He shed His blood to make things right. The gospel of love is my Holy Lamb. My gospel of love is the Great I Am. My gospel of love is the Risen Lamb. My gospel of love is my righteous son who gave His life for everyone. My gospel of love is my holy choice. Listen to Him and hear my voice. My gospel of love is my Holy Seed. I sowed Him in the earth to meet all of your needs. His holy hands made everything. He caused the bells of freedom to ring. This nation is blind and has lost its way, out of darkness into day. My gospel of love won't let you down. He reaches all the way to the ground. My gospel of love is filled with my blood. My gospel of love will calm the floods. My gospel of love made the land and the sea. My gospel of love came out of me. My gospel of love rules the day and the night. My gospel of love will make you wise. My gospel of love will heal your eyes. My gospel of love knows the great and small. My gospel of love belongs to all. My gospel of loves brings peace and joy to every little boy and girl.

My gospel of love is holy and true. My gospel of love is calling you. He's calling you and me to stand and lift every fallen man and bathe them with his holy love that only comes from up above. He reaches deep into the soul and cause His love to take control and bring peace and joy into the mind, erasing doubt and bringing faith in line. Faith and hope are a part of me, that will always set the captives free. My gospel of love is holy and true. My gospel of love is calling you and me to stand and lift up every fallen man, every woman, every boy, and every girl who ever comes into the world.

My gospel of love is my Holy Son who I sent to die for everyone. I sent Him down to set men free when He shed blood on Calvary. Believe in Him and come to me. My gospel of love always honors me, and those who receive Him, there is victory. You must open your heart to my Holy Son who gave His life for everyone. It's written in John 3:16 and John 1:1, believe in Him and come to me through my Son. My Holy Son who will set you free from sin, death, hell, disease, and pain. He will heal your body and also your brain. He's someone who doesn't have to be explained.

My gospel of love is Jesus Christ, the source of all living, and the seed of all life. He's the Alpha and Omega, the first and the last. The beginning and the end. Make Him your choice! He's better than a friend.

"Jesus is my gospel of love."

A Song

You're my Lord, and you're my Savior, my Redeemer, and my Creator. I adore you. I adore you, and I praise your holy name. Lord, you saved me, and you kept me. You are with me every day. You are with me every day. You're my Lord and my Savior, my Redeemer, and my Creator. I adore you, I adore you. Lord, I praise your holy name.

Jesus

Jesus is the rose,
Jesus is the lamb,
Jesus was sent by the Great I Am.
Jesus is the bread,
Jesus is the light,
Jesus is the one that shines so bright,
Jesus is the water,
Jesus is the word,
Jesus is the one that should be heard.
Jesus is the shepherd,
Jesus is the king,
Jesus's holy hands made everything,
Jesus is God's love sent from above.
When John baptized him,
On his shoulder was a dove.
Jesus is the rock,
Jesus is the seed,
Jesus is the lamb,
That had to bleed.
Jesus shed his blood for you and me,
He arose from the dead and set us free.

Who Is This Great Master?

Who gives the abundant life? You may have just guessed it. His name is Jesus Christ. Who is this man called Jesus? He is the Holy Son of God sent by His Holy Father to deliver His holy love. He is the living word of God. He has His Holy body, flesh, and blood. He shed His holy blood on Calvary's cross and died for you and me. This is the part of the Master's plan that set the captives free. Free from doubt, and death, and fear. We have the victory.

In the Master's Hand

In the center of my Master's hand, I have no fear or doubt. As long as His love holds me there, no one can pluck me out. As long as I can receive His love, as He gives it unto me, I am instructed by Him to share it with you. Because His love is really free. As long as I obey His holy voice, my way is clear to see. How to use His holy love to set the captives free. Free from doubt, death, and disease; it enters the human brain, mind, and releases health, and wealth, and peace, and joy. Just a part of His great design.

The Words of Love

The words of love, morning, noon, and also night. For whatever I say is always right. I've made my voice so very clear, so say to others just what you hear. I'm healing your body, soul, and mind. Your eyes so you will never be blind. You'll now see things you've never seen before because I've planted my holy seed in you to see what's old and also new.

I Am My Love

I am my love, and it doesn't put down. I am my love and doesn't frown. I am my love, and my love lifts up. I am my love, and it's a special cup. I always decide who should pick it up. If I choose you to do it, please don't lay it down. The cup that I give you must not touch the ground. The cup that I give is filled with my love. It came down to earth from heaven above. I drank from the cup that my Father gave me. The cup that I drank set the captives free. Without God's love, I wouldn't be where I am today.

The King of Kings

My mind is searching for the King whose holy hands made everything, who put the moon and sun in place so time would never have to race. He made time for you and I so we would have something to go by. He made the night before the day so we would always know the way. Out of darkness into light and meet His Son who is the light—the light that shines into my soul and let His love take full control. He wakes me up each morning to a bright and a brand-new day and gives me words of comfort as I walk along the way.

New Instructions for Your Life

I'm giving you new instructions for your life. Don't ever try to say anything to impress anyone with what you know. Be yourself. Always keep me and my holy word first in your daily activities. I want you to be very conscious of your thoughts and deeds on a daily basis and get into a more dedicated study and prayer life. Seek me early and sincerely. I have you in my hands; my hands are still on your life. Always do what I called you to do first. Your wife needs to know the plans I have for you both of you. You are a successful man of God, and she is a successful woman of God. Continue to work together.

The Voice of God

Jesus is His spokesman.
Jesus is His choice.
Jesus is His Holy Son.
Jesus has His voice.

Have you ever heard the voice of God? He is saying unto me, "Speak the words of God each day and set the captives free." Men need to hear about the Lord each and every day. They need to hear His holy word so they will know the way out of darkness into light and learn His holy way. Jesus knows our minds, and Jesus knows our hearts. Jesus knows our bodies each and every part.

It is the very love of God, His holy seed and Son who was sent to shed His holy blood and die for everyone. He is the resurrection, the way truth, and the life—the source of all that lives eternally because He gave His life. He is the Alpha and Omega, the beginning and the end. He's our Master and our Savior, Jesus Christ our friend. If you'll just accept and receive Him in your heart today, new life He will give you in a new and brand-new way.

He says to me, "You are my son. Not like any other man, but for your life upon this earth, I have a purpose and a plan. I've chosen you to receive and teach my love as I give it into you. It's holy, pure, and righteous, and you know what it can do. It is the most powerful thing within my universe. It kills disease, conquers death, and restores the human mind. It raises the dead and causes the lame to walk and gives site unto the blind."

I Called You

I am the Lord that called you before you were born in your Mother's womb. I called you again when you entered your mother's womb, and I called you again after you came out of your mother's womb. And I am calling you now. My son, write these words:

This letter or word is coming to you who are willing to hear from me again. My name is Jesus. I am looking for children who are willing to obey my voice. Who are willing to learn my ways and follow my instructions? I am coming back to earth very, very soon. Tell everyone that you can. Tell them to begin reading the Word of the Lord, the Seed of Love that came to earth from heaven above. He walked the streets of Galilee and died on the cross for you and me. On the third day he rose again and made the connection between God and man. Jesus is the word of life who took our pain and also strife.

There is a voice that speaks to me. I hear it every day. It comes from the very throne of God in a very special way. The words are clear, and pure, and plain that come to me from Him. I cannot doubt the voice I hear because I hear it every day. It flows from the mouth of our Holy King in a very special way. He whispers very softly into my heart and my mind the words of joy, peace, and hope that no one else could design.

Holy Spirit

Holy Spirit! I love you.
Holy Spirit! I love you.
Holy Spirit! I need you.
Holy Spirit! I need you.
Holy Spirit! I want you.
Holy Spirit! I want you.
Holy Spirit! I adore you.
Holy Spirit! I adore you.
Holy Spirit! I want you to lead me.
Holy Spirit! I want you to lead me.
Holy Spirit! I want you to keep me.
Holy Spirit! I want you to keep me.
Why don't you seek ye
First the kingdom of God?
Why don't you see ye
First the kingdom of God
And his righteousness,
And his righteousness?
And all these things
And all these things
Shall be added unto you
Shall be added unto you!

Holy Spirit, Holy Spirit

Holy Spirit, Holy Spirit, I've been tricked before.
Holy Spirit, I know you know more.
Holy Spirit, Holy Spirit, you always know the way.
Holy Spirit, Holy Spirit, please show me today.
Holy Spirit, Holy Spirit, you are always right.
Holy Spirit, Holy Spirit, lead me day and night.
Holy Spirit, Holy Spirit, won't you be my guide?
Holy Spirit, Holy Spirit, please, Sir, take my pride.
Holy Spirit, Holy Spirit, come into my life.
Holy Spirit, Holy Spirit, lead me with your light.

You Are the Lord

You are the Lord that healeth me,
You are the Lord that set me free.
Your holy blood was shed for me,
You are the Lord that healeth me.
You are the Lord that give me sight,
I'll praise your name both day and night.
You are the Lord that health me,
You are the Lord who set me free.
Oh, Lord, I love to praise your name; your love for me will never change.
It was your love you gave to me
When you shed your blood on Calvary.
You are the Lord that healeth me,
You are the Lord that set me free, and now I have victory.
You are the Lord that set me free.

Jesus, Jesus, Jesus!

Jesus, Jesus, Jesus, come into my heart,
Jesus, Jesus, Jesus, for a brand-new start.
Jesus, Jesus, Jesus, you're the only Son,
Jesus, Jesus, Jesus and the Holy One.
Jesus, Jesus, Jesus, you shed your blood for me,
Jesus, Jesus, Jesus, that's what you set me free.

Lord, I Love You

Lord, I love you,
Lord, I love you,
There is no one up above you.
You're so holy,
You're so righteous,
You're so gracious,
You're so kind,
You're my Lord,
You're my Savior.
Lord, I have you on my mind.

Who Is God?

Who is God? Jesus is God.

Who is God? God is love.

Who is love? Jesus is love.

What is love? Love is God's gift to all mankind.

The source of all life, love is the Holy Seed of God Himself—Jesus, His Holy Son.

God planted his holy seed

Jesus, His Holy Lamb down.

Below the earth, before the foundation was laid, He was slain by God. This set everything in perfect order for the world and ages of time to be made.

So in the beginning, God prepared, formed, fashioned, and created the heavens and the earth through his Son. His word, his love, personified by the word of the Lord, were the heavens made and all of the host of them. By the breath of his mouth, the voice of the Father is the Son. The love of the Father is the Son. The breath of the Father is the Son. And the Father and the Son are one. Since God created everything through His love, Jesus—it cannot be destroyed by man. Why? Because God made everything.

Jesus, Jesus, Jesus Part II

Jesus, Jesus, Jesus, come into my heart,
Jesus, Jesus, Jesus, for a brand-new start.
Jesus, Jesus, Jesus, you're the only Son,
Jesus, Jesus, Jesus and the Holy One.
Jesus, Jesus, Jesus, you shed your blood for me,
Jesus, Jesus, Jesus, that's what set me free.

My Word

"My word is your life and my word is free. I am in you and you are in me" (John 17:1).

"Eat my word which is my flesh and bread and live through me" (John 6:57).

I am my word, and my word is in you. I am my word, and my word is in you. I am my word, and my word is true. My word is old and also new. Since my word is ageless and my word is free—by eating my word, you've become like me. Since I am the one who let you know, my love is in you, and I told you so.

Why Not?

Why not choose the one who knows which way the river really flows?

Who can stop the wind at his spoken word because His voice is always heard?

When you speak with the breath that He gives you from the words of life that are always true, He will impart His spirit to the words received and give the power to be believed.

Who always knows what's best for you and shows you things that you can do to lift up every fallen soul and let His Spirit take control.

Jesus is the only way to the Father's throne. He will show you with His love how to lead the captives home.

I Am My Love

I am my love, and my love is me,
I am my love, and my love is free.
I am my love, and my love is right,
I am my love, and my love is sight.
I am my love, and my love needs you,
I am my love, and my love is true.
I am my love, and my love reaches all,
I am my love, and my love cannot fall.
I am my love, and my love is pure,
I am my love, and my love will always endure.

My Voice

I have given you what you have requested from me, the love that comes directly from me. My love will set the captives free. My love is delivered to you each day so you will always know what to do and say.

You will never hear a voice like mine—holy, pure, and so divine. I've ordained you to teach and preach what you learn from me. It will cause the dumb to speak and the blind to see. Whatever you hear me say to you, it's exactly what I want you to do. Holy Spirit and our Lord Jesus Christ.

My Son, you will always hear my voice. You will always hear me plain and clear because I have given you an open ear, an ear that doesn't receive doubt or fear. Fear is the spirit that transmits lies. Fear is the spirit that blinds the eyes. I've touched your mouth, tongue, and lips, my Son, so you will never lie to anyone. I have also anointed your fingers, eyes, hands, and a head. I'm commanding to heal the sick and raise the dead.

The Words of Love

I've chosen you to speak my voice so you can make the righteous choice. To say just what I say to you. Because what I say is always true. Don't even try to figure it out; for if you do, then in comes doubt, death, and then disease. With these things, I'm never pleased. Just speak whatever you hear me say each and every single day.

The Love of God

The love of God is clean and pure—it helps the weeping heart endure the things that challenge the human mind that causes men to resign. But the love of God, by its purity, is able to set the captives free from the one who tries to take control to steal the body and the soul.

Won't you listen to the voice of Him who made the water in which you drink and swim? He made the birds that fly and sing and causes the bells of freedom to ring. So every heart must accept His love, sent to us from heaven above.

Won't you listen to the voice of our Holy King whose holy hands made everything? He became a servant for you and me and shed His blood at Calvary. Just hear His voice and be set free. He cleans the heart and heals the mind. He raises the dead and gives sight to the blind. He's your friend and also mine. The love of God is pure and sound. It reaches all the way to the ground. It touches the heart and soul of man and gives him strength to understand. It also enters the human mind and takes the blindness from the blind. It reaches deep down in the soul and lets the spirit take control.

The love of God knows you and me. He's the one who set the captives free. The love of God is Jesus Christ our King whose holy hands made everything. His Father sent Him into the earth. He came to us in a holy birth. He walked the streets of Galilee and shed His blood for you and me.

The Lord Is Speaking Clear to Me

The Lord is speaking clear to me. I hear him every day. His voice is very sweet and plain as I walk along my way. My way does not belong to me; it belongs to my Holy King who gives me the very breath of life and a voice that lets me sing. I love to sing to my Holy King whose hands made everything. He shed His holy blood one day; now the bells of freedom ring. May all the little boys and girls hear the voice of my Holy King and learn to sing to Him each day whose hands made everything.

God's Love

The love of God is clean and pure; it helps the weeping soul endure. It dries up all the tears that fall and helps the racing mind to stall, just enough to hear the King and listen to the children sing the songs of joy, peace, and hope. It cancels death and puts down dope.

Oh, let's hear the bells of freedom ring and listen to the children sing the songs of joy, peace, and hope that cancels death and stamps out dope. Dope kills the mind and starves the soul. It steals the silver and the gold and snatches life out of the soul. The love of God, it cannot hold.

But Jesus came to show the way. His life He gave, a price to pay. He shed His blood on Calvary. Believe in Him and be set free. Jesus is the Holy Son; He gave His life for everyone. He shed His blood for you and me; believe in Him and be set free, and then you'll have the victory. Believe in Jesus, and you will see, the one whose blood has set you free.

Jesus is the holy light that always shines so very bright. He always pushes the darkness back and sets the sinner on the holy track who believes in Him and accepts his way out of darkness into day. He's the bright light that will ever shine; and when it enters the human mind, it brings hope, peace, and joy to every girl and boy, to every woman and every man and also peace to a troubled land.

Love Is the Answer to a Life with God

John 3:16
>Love came to earth through God's own son.
>Love is the answer for everyone.
>Love is pure and love is light,
>Love is holy and love is bright.
>Love is pure and love is clear. There is no darkness

1 John 4:8
>There is no fear

1 Corinthians 13:8
>Love will come through when nothing else will.

It's better than a doctor with his capsule and pill. Love is a joy to the body and soul. It's something that never gets out of control.

Love is the answer to a life with God. It's the light to our path on the road we trod. Love encourages, renews, and lifts. It's one of God's most holy righteous gifts.

You cannot love God, if you don't love man (1 John 4:20–21). This is something we must understand.

I Am My Love

I am my love, and my love is true. My love is holy, and I put it in you. When you were just a little babe, the life I gave you, I decided to save.

When you were inside your mother's womb, I gave you life and not a tomb. Now you're like a broom upon my land. Sweep it within my love and your holy hands.

Your hands are holy because they belong to me. Now, my son, you have been set totally free. I have given you the victory.

I am my love, and my love is me. I am my love, and my love is free. I am my love, and my love is right.

I am my love, and my love is sight. I am my love, and my love needs you. I am my love, and my love is true. I am my love, and my love reaches all. I am my love, and it cannot fall. I am my love, and my love is pure. I am my love; it will always endure.

I am my love, and it doesn't put down. I am my love, and it does not frown. I am my love, and my love lifts up. I am my love, and it's a special cup. I always decide who should pick it up.

If I choose you to do it, please don't lay it down. The cup that I give you must not touch the ground. The cup that I give you is filled with my love. It came down to earth from heaven above. I drank from the cup that my Father gave me. The cup that I drunk set the captives free.

I Am

I am the one who gave you life.

I am the one who took your strife.

I am the one who made you new,

I let you see age 72.

I chose you from your mother's womb,

I gave you life and not the tomb. You're like a broom upon my land—sweep with my love and not your hand.

My love is clean, pure, and bright.

It causes the blind to receive their sight.

It causes the dumb to speak and talk. It causes the lame to run and walk. It causes to dead to rise and stand. It gives life to every man. My love is pure, and strong, and right. It causes you to treat others right. My love is the purest form of light. My love gives you my Holy sight.

My love is a guiding light. My love comes from my holy throne. My love will never leave you alone. My love runs wide and deep and tall.

My love will never let you fall. My love erases all doubt and fear. My love will dry up every tear. My love is just the thing for you. My love is just what makes you new.

I Belong to Him

Jesus knows my mind,
    Jesus knows my heart,
    Jesus owns my body, each and every part.
    My eyes belong to him,
    My hands belong to him,
    My soul belongs to him.
    He paid the prices for me way back on Calvary. And this is why I know He really loves me. He shed His holy blood for me.

He Knows

Jesus knows the hearts of men just how they think and feel. Jesus knows the mind of men, just what is false and real. Jesus came to show the way back to our Father's home. Jesus came to reclaim all that Adam gave way when He came; His presence turned the darkness into daylight of the world.

Jesus knows the way we think and why we act the way we do. Jesus speaks the words of life that makes our hearts pure and true. Jesus teaches us how to think and walk the holy way. He leads us with His holy voice from darkness into the day. Jesus is the light of God that shines into our hearts. Jesus heals the minds of men and all its various parts. Jesus is the love God that lives within my soul.

What He gave for you and I is more precious than silver and gold. He shed His blood at Calvary's cross and paid the price for you and me. Receive these words into your heart, and they will set you free. Jesus is the only one that we really trust because He obeyed His Father's voice and paid the price for us all.

His Voice

My ear is listening to the king whose holy hands made everything—the mountains, lakes, hills, and trees everything that lives and breathes. He made the birds and bees that fly and placed the stars up in the sky. The sun and moon He put in place so time would never have to race.

I can hear his voice as he speaks to me. The things that show me how to see. The one who gives us victory who walked the streets of Galilee and shed his blood for you and me. Jesus is that holy lamb. Jesus is the Great I Am. He's the only one to know. We can meet the Father through His Son who shed His blood for everyone.

His voice is clear and pure and bold. It reaches deep into my soul and tells me things my mouth can't hold. He says to go out and share today all the words that come to you from me. And they will set the captives free. The words of joy, and peace, and hope that cancels death and smothers dope. That tells the boys and girls that play that Jesus is the only way. The way from darkness into light so they'll know how to do what's right.

The holy light is God's own son who shed His blood for everyone. He walked the streets of Galilee and paid the price for you and me. He is God's seed of holy love sent to earth from heaven above. There is no love like the Father's Son who shed His blood for everyone.

The Word of the Lord

The Word of the Lord is holy and just. In the Word of the Lord, you can always trust. In the Word of the Lord, you can find your way out of darkness into day. In the word of the Lord, there is peace and joy for every woman, man, girl, and boy. The Word of the Lord is the holy seed that had to live, die, and also bleed. The Word of the Lord is God's Holy Son that had to die for everyone.

When I spoke to my disciples in the book of John and said, "The words that I speak unto you, they are Spirit and they are life came from my Father and the words that I speak have the power to give life"—tell everyone that I am coming back very, very soon.

—The Lord Jesus

The Gospel of Love

The Gospel of Love is Jesus, my Son, who I sent to die for everyone. The Gospel of Love is Jesus Christ. The Gospel of Love is the source of all life. The Gospel of Love is my Holy Lamb. The Gospel of Love is the Great I Am. The Gospel of Love is my holy choice. Listen to Him and hear my voice.

I Am My Love

I am my love, and my love is right. I am my love, and my love is true. I am my love, and my love needs you. He needs you and me to stand and lift up every fallen man. He needs you and me to share His love, to set the captives free.

I am my love; you cannot die for me my Son, but you can tell people what I have done. I shed my blood at Calvary and that's what really set the captives free. They all got up from their graves and walked upon the earth. This showed the world that I have new birth.

His Voice

Be still and know that I am God. I've chosen you to hear my voice and speak what you hear me say to others you may encounter each and every day. I'll speak very clearly and plainly into your heart the words of peace and joy and hope that come right from my heart my son. You must always keep your spirit open unto my holy voice so you can hear me speak to you and make the righteous choice. This world is changing faster than the righteous choice. The world is changing faster than the mind can understand.

What makes up the world, my son, is each and every man. He wanders from the holy plans I placed within my holy word. He's listing to a stranger's voice not spoken from my word. My word is just what he needs for me to be his guide. I'll build him up with peace and joy and take his selfish pride.

His voice rings pure, clear, and plain as it enters the human mind and brain. His voice, when heard, brings peace and cheer when it enters my listening ear. I can feel His love deep in my soul, and it brings joy and peace I cannot hold. He says, "My son, I've chosen you to do some things I want you to.

"I want you to preach and teach about my holy love that I sent to earth from heaven above. Jesus is my love my Holy Son and Lamb. Jesus is the Great I Am. I sent Him down into the earth to give all men a brand-new birth. Keep listening to my voice, my son, and share my love with everyone. Men must hear my voice through you so they will always know what's true. Don't say a thing you don't hear me say so they will walk the holy way. The way to the Father is through the Son who gave His life for everyone.

"Jesus walked the streets of Galilee and shed His blood for you and me. The day that He was crucified, the debt for sin was satisfied. He glorified the Father at Calvary, and His blood set the captives free.

"Jesus is the only way out of darkness into day. Jesus knows the hearts of men, just how they think and feel. Jesus knows the minds of men both what is false and real. Jesus says, 'Come into me and obey my holy word and listen to my voice,' and you see its one they've never heard. They listen to the voice of men who do not speak for me because they don't know it was my blood that set the captives free.

"Men do not know me as their Savior and Lord. They do not know me as the Son of God. They do not know me as the Lamb who was slain before the foundation of the world was laid. They do not know me as the King of kings and Lord of lords. They do not know me as the first and last.

"They do not know me as the seed of the woman in Genesis 3:15. They do not know me as the burning bush. They do not know me as the true source of the tree of life. They do not know me as the bread of life. They do not know me as the living word. They do not know me as the word of God. They do not know me as the living water. They do not know me as the resurrection and the life. They do not know me as the light of the world. They do not know me as the well that never runs dry. They do not know me as I want to know them. They know my word but not me."

The King

My soul is searching for the King who causes the bells of freedom to ring. My soul is searching for the King whose holy hand made everything. My mind is guided by the King whose teaching me why He made everything that lives and breathes—the mountains, and lakes, and hills, and trees. He made the sun to shine so bright and caused the day to follow night (Gen. 1:8). He walked the streets of Galilee and shed His blood for you and me. This is what set the captives free, and now we have the victory.

The King's name is Jesus Christ. The one who made the sacrifice. The battle over sin and death is won because the Father gave His Holy Son and paid the price for everyone. Now Jesus came to show the way, out of darkness and into day. He is the holy bread of life who took our pains and also strife. Won't you listen to His holy voice so you can make the righteous choice?

Who, What, When, Where, How, Why of God

John 1. In the beginning [before all time] was the word (Christ) and the word was with God, and the word was God himself [1a]

2. He was present originally with God

3. All things were made and came into existence through Him; and without Him was not even one thing made that has come into being

4. In Him was life and the life was the light of me 1:8 No man has ever seen God at any time; the only unique Son or the only begotten God who is in the bosom [in the intimate presence of the Father] He has declared Him [He has revealed him and brought Him out where he can be seen. He has interpreted Him and He has made Him known.]

What Is God?

"He who does not love has not become acquainted with God [does not and never did now him] For God is love," says 1 John 4:8. What is love? John 3:16 says love is God's greatest gift to all mankind. The source of all life. Love is the holy seed of God Himself. Jesus is Holy Son. The love of God is the most powerful force in the universe. It is more powerful than all the explosives in the world put together in one place to go off. When it explodes, it destroys nothing but death, disease, evil, anger, hatred, sin, doubt, fear, etc.

I Belong to Him

His holy word is true. He also died for you. Won't you trust him now? Now's the time to choose; Him you cannot lose. Jesus is the one only living Son. He's the better choice. Listen to His voice. He's saying, "I love you, won't you come to me? I will set you free. I am my Father's love sent from heaven above. Jesus is my name.

"Won't you come to me? You'll have the victory that I have won for you. I'll breathe into your soul and let your heart take hold of things you've never known. Just say *yes* to me, and I will set you free. And you'll never be alone."

He controls each day and time. Jesus knows my heart and mind. He's the one who gives me sight, out of darkness and into light. Light and darkness cannot be sold. Jesus always has control. Light flows from His holy throne. Light belongs to Him alone. His light is pure, and clean, and clear. It flows so freely into my ear and opens my eyes so I can see the things that really belong to me.

From Me to You

I am life, and life is free. I gave my love to set you free. He shed his blood at Calvary. The blood He shed came out of me. I'm His Father, and He's my Son. He came to die for everyone. Everyone who believes in Him will learn to walk and talk like Him. They will hear His voice and speak His word. The clearest voice they'll ever heard. The voice they'll hear comes right from me. The son who gives them victory. My voice brings joy and peace and hope. It cancels death and smothers dope.

From Me to You Part II

My great love is sent to you so you will always know what's true. I'll take your pains, your stress, and strife and give to you my brand-new life. Please open up your heart to me so I can set your spirit free. I've given you what's on my heart so you can have a brand-new start. I'm blessing you, my son, today with words of love that come your way.

Jesus chose twelve men to be His disciples. He asked them to follow Him and would make them fishers of men. He showed them how to fish for men. He used His love as the bait. Jesus revealed Himself and His Father to the twelve disciples. He taught them how to love one another and their enemies. He gave them the purpose and the plan of salvation. He also let them know He was going to die and rise from the dead in three days. Jesus is the love of God in the flesh.

God's Love

God loves man so much, He sent His Jesus to die for them. But God hates sin. Why? Because sin separates man from God. Jesus came to earth to bring man back to God. How? By revealing God to all mankind. How? By signs and miracles, telling everyone about His Father. Dying on the cross and rising from the dead and conquering sin and death. He is the resurrection and the life.

On the third day, He got up from the grave, conquering sin and death. Why did Jesus die on the cross for you and me? Because this was the command from His Father. Why was it so important for Jesus to die and become sin for us? Because God needed Jesus to bring us back to Him after we were separated from God by Adam when He sinned in the Garden of Eden.

When Adam sinned after his separation from God spiritually, every man, woman, boy, and child born into this world was born a sinner. Sin can only be removed by the shedding of holy blood. Jesus was the only person qualified to do what God needed to be done. Jesus Christ took our place by becoming sin for you and I on the cross. At the moment that He said, "My God, my God, why have you forsaken me?" He was separated from His Father for a split second. Immediately after that, He was received as a payment to God for our sin. This was God's way of having His Son redeem us.

But how do we become children of God? John 3:16 says it completely: "For God so love the world"—meaning, all mankind that whosoever believes in His only Begotten Son shall not perish but have everlasting life.

John 3:17 says, "For God sent not his son into the world to condemned to world but that the world through Him might be saved."

Romans 10:9–13 tells us how we are saved:

That if thou shall confess with thy mouth the Lord Jesus and believe in thine hart that God hath raised him from the dead, thou shall be saved

For with the heart man believeth unto righteousness and with the mouth confession is made unto salvation

For the scripture saith, whosoever believeth on him shall not be ashamed

For there is no difference between the Jew and the Greek: for the same Lord over all is rich unto all that call upon Him

For whosoever shall call upon the name of the Lord shall be saved.

About the Author

Oliver F. Fultz was born in St. Louis, Missouri, to Nathan and Lena Mae Fultz. He was a licensed and ordained minister of The Gospel Christian Faith Center Church in 1996 and today handles the baptisms. As a member of the Boy Scouts of America for forty-seven years and three years as a scout executive, he served with the United State Marine Corps as well. After twenty-eight years of working for the US Postal Service, he retired.

He graduated from John Marshall Elementary in 1946 and Washington Tech High in 1960. Following high school, he went on to graduate from Mound City Business College in 1962 and the Institute for Boy Scouts in March 1967 and John F. Kennedy Special Warfare Center for the US Army.

He has been married to Delores Fultz for thirty-four years now, both serving in the Ministry of Christian Faith Center Church.

CPSIA information can be obtained
at www.ICGtesting.com
Printed in the USA
JSHW052322130920
7841JS00002B/91

9 781098 047535